Living on the Edge

Alison Sage

OXFORD
UNIVERSITY PRESS

OXFORD
UNIVERSITY PRESS

Great Clarendon Street, Oxford OX2 6DP

Oxford University Press is a department of the University of Oxford.
It furthers the University's objective of excellence in research, scholarship,
and education by publishing worldwide in

Oxford New York
Auckland Bangkok Buenos Aires Cape Town Chennai
Dar es Salaam Delhi Hong Kong Istanbul Karachi Kolkata
Kuala Lumpur Madrid Melbourne Mexico City Mumbai
Nairobi São Paulo Shanghai Taipei Tokyo Toronto

Oxford is a registered trade mark of Oxford University Press
in the Uk and in certain other countries

Published in the United Kingdom
by Oxford University Press

First published 2001
10 9 8 7 6 5 4

British Library Cataloguing in Publication Data

Data available

ISBN 0 19 917388 5
Available in packs
People of Different Lands Pack of Four (one of each book) ISBN 0 19 917390 7
People of Different Lands Class Pack (six of each book) ISBN 0 19 917391 5

Printed in Hong Kong

Acknowledgements

The Publisher would like to thank the following for permission to reproduce
photographs: B & C Alexander: pp 5, 6 (top), 8 (top), 10 (top), 11 (middle and bottom),
23 (top); B & C Alexander/Anne Hawthorne: pp 12 (bottom), 13 (top), 22 (centre);
Christine Osborne Pictures: pp 14 (bottom), 18 (top and bottom right); Corel: pp 3, 4
(top), 8 (bottom), 9 (top), 10 (centre and bottom), 13 (bottom right), 16 (left), 17, 19
(top), 21 (bottom right), 23 (bottom); Hutchison Picture Library/Pern: p. 7; Hutchison
Picture Library/Jeremy Horner: p. 19 (bottom); Oxford Scientific Films/Rick Price: p. 13
(bottom left); Panos Pictures/Caroline Penn: pp 6 (bottom), 14 (middle); Panos Pictures;
p. 15 (top); Panos Pictures/Giacomo Parozzi: p. 16 (right); Panos Pictures/John Miles: p. 18
(middle left); Panos Pictures/Paul Smith p. 19 (top); Panos Pictures/Jon Spaull: p. 21
(bottom left); Popperfoto: p. 22 (top); Robert Harding/Geoff Renner: p. 12 (top); Robert
Harding/I Griffiths: p. 15 (bottom); Still Pictures/Peter Frischmuth; p. 4 (bottom); Still
Pictures/Michael Sewell p. 9 (bottom); Still Pictures/Julio Etchart/Reportage: p. 20; Tony
Stone Images/Chris Arend: p. 11 (top); Tony Stone Images/Michael Setbaun: p. 21
(centre); Tony Stone Images/Kevin Schafer: p. 22 (bottom).

Maps and globes by Geo Atlas

Illustrations by: Petra Röhr-Rouéndaal (p. 17)

Front cover photograph by Corel

Contents

Introduction

People are not spread evenly throughout the world. Although nearly 6 billion people are now living on Earth, only about 10% of the land is suitable for human settlement.

Water covers more than two-thirds of the Earth's surface. Most of the land is too cold, dry, high or too poor quality to live on.

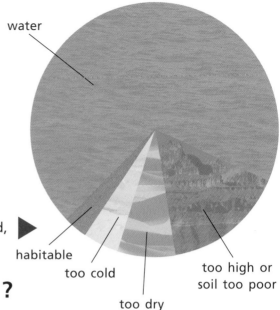

water

habitable

too cold

too dry

too high or soil too poor

Where does everyone live?

About half the world's people live in towns or cities. Most other people live on a surprisingly small part of the globe. There are huge areas of the Earth where no one lives.

Most people want to live where the climate is not too harsh, where they can find food easily and make homes for their families.

But even today, when it is possible to fly from London to New York in an afternoon, there are still people who live in places that seem both difficult and dangerous. How do they do it? Can we learn some lessons in survival from them?

Could you live through an Arctic winter or a hot, dry summer in the Sahara?

Survival!

Everyone needs:

- food
- water
- shelter
- to keep in contact with other people.

Where people live

The **Inuit** live in the Arctic where it always freezes in winter.

North America

London •
Paris •

• New York

The place with the highest snowfall is Mount Rainier, Washington state, USA. As much as 15 metres of snow may fall there in one year.

• Mexico City

The Sahara Desert is the hottest place in the world. Temperatures can rise as high as 58°C.

South America

• Rio de Janeiro

Where do most people live in cities?

[Bar chart showing % of people living in cities by continent:
North America: 70
South America: 70
Europe: 70
Africa: 30
Asia: 30
Australasia: 80]

% of people living in cities (y-axis: 0 to 100)

Continents (x-axis)

The Tuareg live in a hot, dry part of Africa.

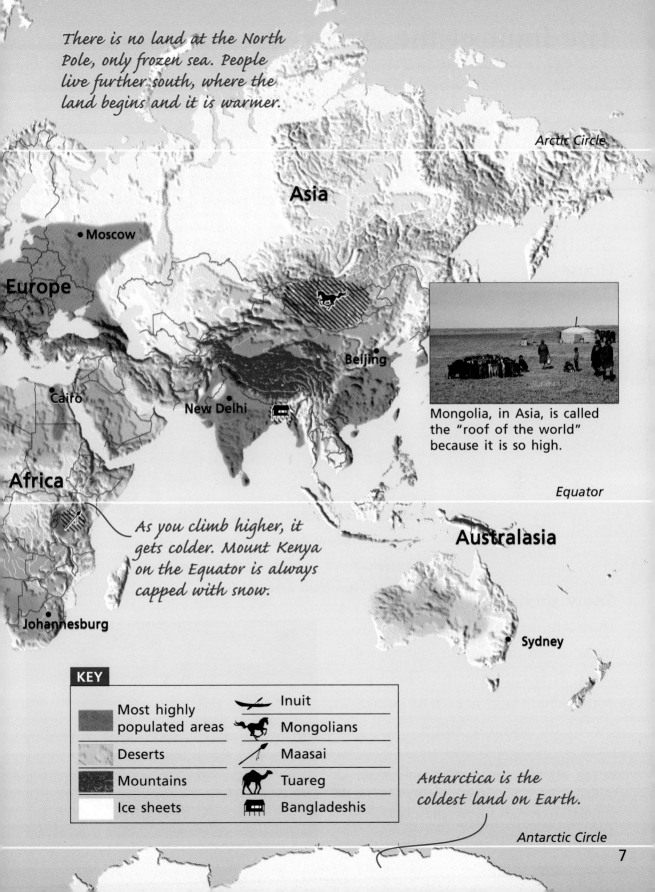

There is no land at the North Pole, only frozen sea. People live further south, where the land begins and it is warmer.

Asia

• Moscow

Europe

Beijing

Cairo

New Delhi

Africa

Mongolia, in Asia, is called the "roof of the world" because it is so high.

Equator

As you climb higher, it gets colder. Mount Kenya on the Equator is always capped with snow.

Australasia

Johannesburg

• Sydney

KEY

Most highly populated areas	Inuit
Deserts	Mongolians
Mountains	Maasai
Ice sheets	Tuareg
	Bangladeshis

Antarctica is the coldest land on Earth.

The Inuit of the Arctic

The **Inuit** people live north of the Arctic Circle in Canada. Survival is a challenge here: winter temperatures often fall below −40°C – that is more than twice as cold as the average deep-freeze.

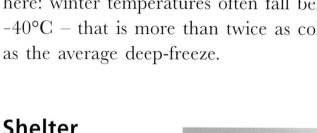

North Pole
Greenland
Canada

Shelter
Houses

The porch stops heat being lost when the door is opened.

Houses must be raised up from the permafrost – otherwise it would melt and they would sink!

Snow shelters

Inuit children are taught how to make a simple shelter out of soft snow. It is called a quinzhee and could save their lives if they are out in the open at night.

In the winter, Inuit hunters sometimes build an igloo as a temporary shelter. It takes an expert to cut and place the blocks of firm snow.

Cabins and tents

In the summer the Inuit often travel to the Arctic coast to fish and hunt whales. They live in wooden cabins or tents. The tents were once made from sealskin, but today they are usually made of artificial fibres.

▲ A camp on the Arctic Circle. It is summer and people are living in tents, but there is still plenty of ice.

Keeping warm

Some Inuit clothes are still made in the traditional way – from animal skins. The fur is turned inwards to trap the air and **insulate** people against the cold.

Caribou skin parkas

Kamiks (fur boots)

Did you know?
- Snow can insulate you against the bitter wind.
- There are hundreds of different kinds of snow.

The Inuit eat lots of fat to help keep them warm. Fish and fat also provide extra vitamins which the Inuit need because they don't eat many vegetables.

9

Everything has its use

Today, the **Inuit** don't depend on hunting and fishing alone. But the Arctic creatures are still very important to them. Every part of a fish, caribou or seal will be used – nothing is wasted.

Some animals have found ways to survive the extreme cold. Seals have a thick layer of fat, called **blubber**, to keep them warm.

▲ Every part of this walrus will be used by the hunters and their families.

◄ A seal must come up for air. This is when a patient hunter – or a polar bear – can catch it.

Polar bears look cuddly but they can be very dangerous. They are the largest meat-eating animals on land. The Inuit hunt them for their fur and meat – but their liver is poisonous to humans.

Celebrations

After weeks of winter darkness, the Inuit celebrate the return of the Sun with dogsled racing, shooting contests, seal-skinning, and even tea-making competitions.

In the summer, when it never gets dark, time by the clock tends to be less important. Festivals are often still in full swing at 4 o'clock in the morning.

At festivals, such as this blanket toss ceremony in Alaska, people can meet up and swap news. ▶

Keeping in touch

In winter, the Inuit used to travel over the ice by dogsled. Today, they use **snowmobiles** or **skidoos**.

In summer, when the rivers melt, they often use a single-person canoe called a **kayak**.

▲

An Inuit family on a skidoo

◀ Inuit children go to school like any other Canadians. They spend time on the Internet, getting in touch with the rest of the world.

Antarctica, the coldest land on Earth

Antarctica is a giant island. Its only visitors are scientists, explorers, and a few tourists. No one lives here because it is much too cold.

South Pole

Seals and penguins live in the seas around Antarctica, but even they cannot cope with winter at the South Pole. Here, temperatures can fall as low as -89°C during the months of darkness.

◀ A seal sits on an ice floe in the lonely Antarctic landscape.

There is little **pollution** at the South Pole, so it is perfect for studying:

- the stars
- tiny plants in the ice – these may have been among the very first living things on Earth.

The clear Antarctic air is perfect for looking at the stars. This telescope has been built with heaters which melt the ice that builds up on it.

How to survive in the Antarctic

Keep head covered (25% of heat is lost from the head).

Put petroleum jelly up nose to stop delicate skin from drying out and cracking in the bitter wind.

Wear lots of thin layers of clothing to keep warm.

▲
How scientists and explorers survive

Animals must **adapt** to the extreme cold.

Ice fish

The ice fish is transparent and lives at the bottom of the sea. A natural substance in its body acts like antifreeze.

Emperor penguin

This bird is clumsy on land but is a brilliant swimmer. It has the largest body of all sea birds. Its thick **blubber** acts as insulation. If an Emperor penguin runs, it overheats and has to jump into the sea to cool down.

Desert survivors – the Tuareg

The hot, dry desert is another challenge to survival. In summer, daytime temperatures rise to over 40°C, but can fall to near freezing at night. And for months, even years, there may be no rain at all.

The Tuareg people are **nomads**. They move from one part of the Sahara Desert to another with their camels, donkeys, and goats, looking for fresh grazing land. The animals provide food, transport, and can even be sold for cash in an emergency.

Equator

Each kind of animal grazes in a different way. This means there should be enough food for them all. ▶

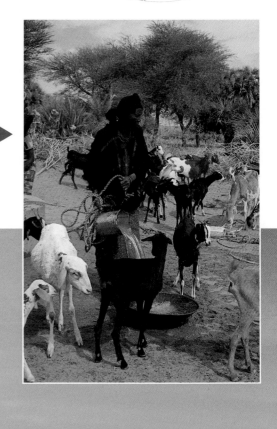

Shelter

The Tuareg live in tents – these have to be carried everywhere, so they must be light.

A family can pack their home on the backs of two camels.

Tuareg people make strangers welcome. In the desert, you never know when you will need help yourself.

Camels

Camels are well adapted to the desert.

Stores food in its hump – this gets bigger or smaller depending on how well fed the camel is.

Long eyelashes protect eyes from sun and sand.

Can close nostrils – useful in a sandstorm

Large feet, for walking on sand

Tough lips can chew spiky thorn bushes.

Life on the plain – the Maasai

The **Maasai** live on grasslands in East Africa. They move with their cattle to find new grass every dry season and return when the rains arrive. For them, their cattle are the most important thing in the world. "I hope your cattle are well?" is the Maasai way of saying, "How are you?"

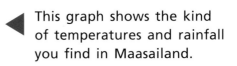

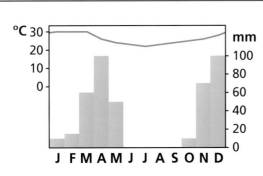

This graph shows the kind of temperatures and rainfall you find in Maasailand.

Maasai men and boys keep the cattle safe. Their zebu cattle have small humps rather like camels. This helps them to survive where there is little water.

In order to be treated as a grown-up, a Maasai boy used to kill a lion by himself. Today this rarely happens, but Maasai boys are still very independent.

Women take charge of house-building. The most important day in a girl's life is when she makes her own house.

Houses are covered with mud and cow dung which makes them stay cool inside in the hot, dry season.

Small high windows let out smoke from a small fire.

Narrow doorway

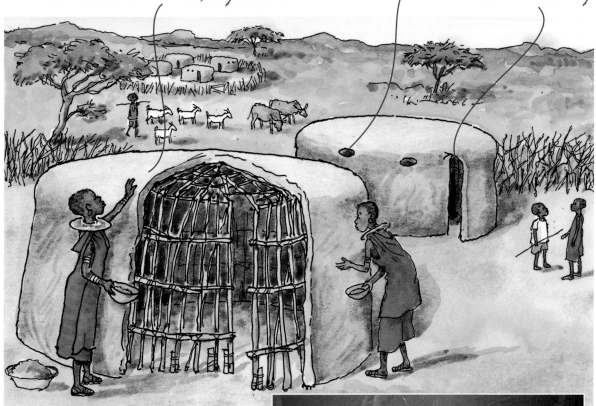

▲ A group of houses is surrounded by thorn bushes to keep people and cattle safe from wild animals.

Maasai people travel mostly on foot. Sometimes women have to walk up to 25 km a day to collect water.

▲ Inside a Maasai home

Staying cool
At home

People in hot countries have learned how to keep cool, using materials around them.

▲ Houses in hot countries often have a **verandah** where people can sit outside in the shade.

▲ Thick mud walls **insulate** these houses in San'a, Yemen – they are warm in winter and cool in summer. In other places, some people live in caves, or even underground, for the same reason.

▲ The Ancient Egyptians built wind scoops on top of their houses to catch the breeze and cool the house. Today, in Dubai, United Arab Emirates, wind towers on houses work in the same way.

In Japan, bamboo screens keep out the Sun's glare. Some houses have removable walls, so the house can be opened in the summer and closed in the winter.

Cool customs

In hot countries, people:

- work in the cool mornings and evenings, and sleep in the hot afternoons – this is known as "taking a siesta" in Spain

- wear long, light, loose garments, often in several layers, which cover the body and **insulate** the wearer against the hot Sun

- eat food that is dried or preserved (like raisins, nuts, or yoghurt) because fresh food does not keep well in the heat.

This man wears loose, pale-coloured clothes and a turban to protect his head from the heat.

Dried food on sale in a market in Aswan, Egypt.

People everywhere like to stay cool with an ice-cream!

Water everywhere –
char-dwellers of Bangladesh

In some places there is too much water.

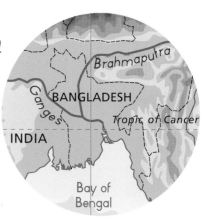

In Bangladesh, hundreds of thousands of people live with the constant fear of being washed away. The huge River Brahmaputra often floods, and the danger is greater when storms strike in the Bay of Bengal.

Some people live on small islands actually in the river, called chars. These are always changing shape and can even disappear when the river floods.

People grow rice because rice needs a lot of water.

These houses are quick to build and easy to move. A house can be built in a couple of days.

People build their houses on wooden stilts to keep them above the flood waters.

On top of the world – living in Mongolia

In the high, flat country of Mongolia it is very hot in summer and very cold in winter. People live in sheltered valleys in the freezing winters and move higher up with their animals in the hot, dry summers.

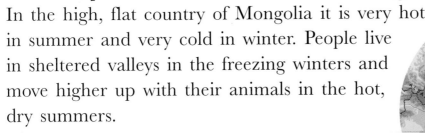

A yurt is a tent. It is traditionally made of felt hung over a frame.

There are many different words for "horse" in the Mongolian language.

Mongolians are very proud of their horses, and children ride as soon as they can walk.

The Bactrian camel has two humps.

People keep sheep, goats, horses, camels, and **yak**. They milk all their animals.

In the summer, Mongolians love horse racing, archery, and wrestling competitions.

Yak give milk, butter, meat, wool, and leather.

Tourists and explorers

Often, places that are difficult to live in are also very beautiful. This means people want to visit them.

Explorers want to be the first to climb a mountain or walk across a desert. Some, like Captain Scott on his expedition to the South Pole in 1912, die in the attempt.

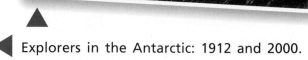

Explorers in the Antarctic: 1912 and 2000.

If there are too many tourists, the wild places will change. Visitors bring **pollution**, and people and even animals suffer as their homes are destroyed to make way for hotels and roads.

We must treat these wild places with respect so they will always be there for everyone to enjoy.

Conclusion

All round the world, people live in difficult and dangerous places. They often cope in very similar ways. They learn from the past, but they also try out new **technologies** and new materials.

Arctic wolves have two layers of fur so they can sleep comfortably in temperatures of −40°C.

In the morning, a desert snake pokes its head out of its burrow, so that its brain will warm up from 15°C to 25°C – then it is able to think and move.

People – and animals – have to adapt to where they live. They build homes to protect themselves from extreme weather and they learn to find food all year round. Today, even in remote places, people can keep in touch by using the Internet.

Air conditioning was first introduced in AD 650 in Turkey. Water was pumped up to the top of the house and then sprayed down in showers in front of the windows.

Glossary

adapt To change to suit a particular situation.

air conditioning A system to keep air cool in a building.

blubber The layer of fat under the skin of a whale or seal.

insulate To stop heat or electricity escaping from something by covering it with another layer.

Inuit A person or a race of people from the Arctic north of Canada, America, and Greenland.

kayak A covered, narrow canoe with a double-bladed paddle.

Maasai A race of people in Africa who live by herding cattle.

nomads People who move about depending on the time of year, to find food for themselves and their animals.

parka A warm, weatherproof coat with a hood.

permafrost Ground that is permanently frozen, often very deep.

pollution Damage to the environment caused by human activities.

snowmobile or **skidoo** A small, open motor vehicle for travelling on snow.

technology The use of science to do something practical.

verandah A platform around the outside of a house, often with a roof.

yak A long-haired ox.

yurt A circular tent made from a framework of poles covered by felt or skins. Yurts are the traditional houses of the Mongolians.

Index